the flap pamphlet series

Sikiliza

T0346954

open, read, turn

Sikiliza

the flap pamphlet series (No. 31)
Printed and Bound in the United Kingdom

Published by the flap series, 2023
the pamphlet series of flipped eye publishing
All Rights Reserved

Cover Design by Petraski
Series Design © flipped eye publishing, 2010

Author Photo © Kojo Apeagyei, 2019
First Edition

ISBN-13: 978-1-905233-82-3

Supported using public funding by
ARTS COUNCIL
ENGLAND
LOTTERY FUNDED

Sikiliza

Bella Cox

for hearts that yearn and hearts that leap

Contents | *Sikiliza*

Your Autobiography Without You in It

The house surrounded by wheat fields has a doorframe with only one height mark notched into it. Your mother still dresses in one colour; a nectarine, a pineapple, a cucumber pushing her trolley down the dairy aisle, still drinking cow's milk. Your sister grows like the wheat, fast, breakable. Maybe older, she still travels. Your mother holds her anger gently, mostly, tucked under the warmth of her tongue; your sister not conjuring it the way you would. They both sing off-pitch in the kitchen. No one plays the piano in the living room. Food in the house is mostly beige. A step-father blooms into the picture, tall and shadowed. There is work and promotions and diets and birthdays and squabbles and journeys and new homes with unmarked doorframes. Perhaps your sister admits she is lonely, but never bored with dogs for company. Your mother would appreciate more advice, more Mother's Day cards. There is no coriander in the chapatis. Do they go on to eat without you?

neither birthplace nor genetics, still home

after Sumia Jaama's 'Before Leaving'

any phone number beginning +254 / is a trip wire / the phone rings loud and long in my hand / the map of the world pulls slowly in or out of focus / I do not answer / the voicemail greeting loops / *samahani, mteja wa nambari uliopiga, hapatikani kwa sasa* / in the kitchen I search for *chapatis* and lost accents / find only crumpets / snow on the window sill / when my new friends call / their phone numbers belong / local status *0* / I answer on the second ring / English can sound so curt and stiff / I say *asante sana* / forget they do not know this tongue on me / all the mangoes here have lost their sweetness / a man on the street points at the shape of Africa / silver around my cream neck / asks if I'm from there / *ndiyo* sounds old in my mouth / the way truths can gather dust when neglected / he tells me of a home I do not share / we find common ground in the red earth he describes / I am thankful / this man does not assume me tourist / some nights in bed / I dial numbers I know will go to voicemail / lull myself into dreams / starlings rising

Hands

You pushed your hair back, same fingers as my first best friend,
didn't smile the same way when I explained that —

You're not the point.

A musical boy I liked to watch play piano once told me
he imagined my hand circling inside his boxers at night.

That's not it either.

I spend years gnawing at nail beds, teeth and nail file ready.
Self-soothing, the therapist told me.

I'm losing you.

A cold-eyed woman I still wish would love me held my palms to hers
proclaimed them *gay hands*, sending me —

In hindsight I guess it's not that funny.

Sweaty hands aren't sexy. Unless yours are hot and want cooling like M's did. Lucky.
When I try, I still feel her firm hand in mine, swinging madly toward school buses.

Was that love, do you think?

I've forgotten the point.

Once, a palm-reader explained my life would be painfully long.
I asked and they searched, but we couldn't find the heart line.

Both hands own scars no one in this poem has kissed.
Crescent moon stories shining pink in the bathwater only for me.

Converging

Love is born into every human being; it calls back the
halves of our original nature together; it tries to make
one out of two and heal the wound of human nature.

- Aristophanes

We meet
                              already interlaced

roots quietly entwined.

My history
            laid out   as if tracing paper
                        over yours.

        Your smile rising before my punchline hits
my eyebrow arching before your tongue meets cheek.

                              Yellowest blue
                        bluest yellow.

        Hold your palm
                to the light
                        trace the lines

        at each feathered junction
                              there I am
                        there
                        we lie.

Floriography

Floriography is the 'language of flowers' and has been practised for thousands of years across different cultures. – Museum Selection

In one, you arrive as a bouquet of purple hyacinths;
a fresh bud for each broken promise, dew-studded
and pleading to be allowed to see me. In another,
there are no words, only your strong arms lifting
me the way Noah lifts Allie in that film, my face
nuzzling your hydrangea-scented chest.
Many times you come; a daisy chain between your teeth
making up for lost time. But most afternoons, your face
is a field of yellow dahlias beaming up at me,
awaiting sunrise,

    and there I stand, interrogating the gold, checking for ants
    or lies. Watching you wait in anticipation at my door
    I can't allow myself to let you in — want nothing more
    than to be a girl running through spring fields, gathering
    every flower to my lips until we are both numb from loving
    ourselves back into the summer we began.
    But reality
                          is slow traffic.
    Reality is wilting alone in an overheated car,
     peering into every passing face, hoping for
      a glimpse of petals that resemble yours.
       Reality is subduing the now-familiar
        stomach ache of missing you
          to wonder again why
            in every fantasy
              no matter the basis,
              no matter the stakes,
                we always end with
                  you, fixed.
                 Me, rooted.
               Every
                almost-
                bloom
                 withered.

Pathology

Dissection is ugly business. Each moment sliced and quartered; atomic slivers. A lingering fistful of hair. An almost-chuckle on the word *don't*. Genuine tears as you held me, or forced? Zoom in. Scalpel. Peel another layer. *Goodbye*. Anguish or relief? I could do this all year. Whole months sacrificed in pursuit of reliving. You'd let me. Haggard and time-worn, dragging my thoughts again through the gore. A frown: confusion or scorn? Blade flash. Every intake of breath is suspect —

All this is hindsight. Even if a prognosis is found, ours is a minced cadaver, love.

HOWL

At work, I hug a man in greeting. In return, he humps me three times. I pinch the back of his neck as if squishing the hard shell of a beetle until he scuttles. Sneers. *Strong woman, huh?* Another day I offer an idea to a team of men. Eight eyes look away until it is adopted by a baritone. A day before, I stand in the shower until the water goes cold, razor in one hand, shout in the other. On the Underground, I watch a woman notice my legs, watch her eyes bulging, watch her unable to blink away. Another evening, walking through a park, a rottweiler man barks that he enjoys the way my body cannot help but jiggle. My jaw stays clenched all day. Navigating a swarm of lurking boys; my heart in my throat, their hands in their pockets, one pre-teen calls after my smile, asks where it is, as if he's earned it. At the pub I cannot laugh at the rape jokes, pretend not to notice eyes roll. My fingernails press half-moons into my palms, I bite my cheeks until they bleed. In bed with a man, he refuses to taste me, says *Hair on a woman's body is unclean.* An hour later, he consumes a furry peach whole. Another night, pretzeled in another pub toilet jamming another door closed with my foot, no one can explain how the lock broke. I stare at the only female bartender. Watch the punters slime around her. The TV news blazes in the background. Another man's DNA has been found crawling inside the body of another unconscious girl. A stone-faced reporter airs questions as to how it got there. As if this is the first time. As if our lives are not connected. As if we should be used to it. I think of my grandmother, of every groaning woman before and after her. Imagine them all rising as one beneath a full moon, loud and unafraid. Today, I reclaim my idea, speak it louder. Snap my razors in half. Lock eyes with the woman on the tube. I rip a growl from my throat for the man on the street, dare him to chase it. Snarl *Fuck you* at the pre-teen, at the jokers, at the shame blushing my own cheeks. Demand the bartenders fix their damn door. I tell the lover to leave. I howl at the TV, at my mirrored face, at the moon who does so much nothing.

Not Marble

Black Out Poem from "Alias Grace" by Margaret Atwood

A surgeon should be human

Deliberately   and delicately   steady

Suffering

the knife.

Men and women   are not marble,

They   become noisy   and   leaky.

mysteries   to be   revealed

Both material   and ethereal

A thousand   shadowy bones

Scattered   like

angels.

December 2011

Golden Shovel after Jake Wild Hall's 'Solomon's World'

Unlit, at night, Diani beach swells to a bruised eye and
my folded arms, pale with entitlement, glow across my
huffing chest watching you march away. Your skin
swallowed by darkness. This New Years' party is
a kaleidoscope doused in rum and we are young lovers in a
feud, sulking, separated by sand when, like a frenzied bullet,
the first *askari* launches at your tangled fro; presumed proof
of drug-dealing. You are 17 and skinny, a boy in a red vest
startled and shrinking under vicious fists. And suddenly I
am running. Wrenching, punching, shrieking that they cannot
arrest you for just being. Snarling, they beat and zip-tie and give
you a warning that leaves a bitterness I taste when I kiss you.

Cracks

A bruise is a squashed egg, sunny side up.
The squashed egg, sunny side up, is an abused woman.
The abused woman is a cityscape in a blackout.

The cityscape in a blackout is a universe with no stars.
The universe with no stars is an eye without spark.
The eye without spark is a child in distress.

The child in distress is a bridge leading nowhere.
The bridge leading nowhere is a forgotten idea.
The forgotten idea is a misfired gun.

The misfired gun is a boy with no courage.
The boy with no courage is known to squash eggs.
To leave them dripping, leave them trembling,

leave them still trying to be sunny side up.

Sister

In the dark I can't remember if it was my back that blistered or yours. The sun-hot edges of a waterslide flare red in my mind but it's your face folding into a whimper. A friend says they don't understand this closeness, not even "full." Your five-year-old eyes wide at my witch's cauldron, our tiny bodies crouching to anything with fur, our palms sweaty with first day nerves holding on tight. Blood pooling around your face on the tarmac, the wheels I could not stop, the hospital I wasn't allowed to visit, the lip stitches I sense in my mouth. You beaming from the front row, across dinner tables, from your lumpy bed. Wide-eyed fixation on my stories, laughing to tears, your joke or mine? Your Post-it notes on leftovers, our tupperware affection. Your small, soft, plummeting body, my raw fingers grasping the air, your panicked eyes, the aching chasm that chars the base of my throat every time I imagine you gone.

> At home, I wait for the timbre of your footfall.
> Listen for your mood in the kettle's switch.

Saltwater Parable

Paella scented. Seawater flecked.
　Skin, the same dusky oil as mine,

hair, long enough to brush his shoulders.
　English: worse than promised.

He taught me to turn my back to the waves,
　said this way, sea salt would not sting my eyes.

Then retreated with the tide, without return,
　as if to test the lesson I'd learnt.

Kelsley

I am on my knees tussling once more
with the buckle of your belt while you
caress a strand of hair from my face,
that look in your eye like you've won the lottery
or seen a mirage, but it's one you love, one
you almost can't believe would visit you like this
and suddenly I've unclasped you,
relishing your gasp as you do that thing
where you pretend I'm doing *you* a favour
and that I don't have to and I give you that look
like you're a feast and I am starving
so you smile, leaning back on your elbows
as we shimmy your jeans to the floor,
the room filling with the scent of you —
nothing else matters but the rhythm of your breathing
and this sweet sour softness I almost can't believe
you've opened for me, and I keep moving,
my face, my fingers, immersed, looking up
to find your eyes liquid deep, piercing, and full
as if meeting mine for the first time
and somewhere outside the moon is growing
fuller higher brighter bolder
like your perfect mouth

Ode to Menstruation

After Victoria Adukwei Bulley's 'What it Means'

…but I have learnt to love this viscous content,
this daily birth into expectant hand, silicone chalice,
this clench-and-release monthly drumbeat,
this slick reminder of the animal in me,

most months tipped into toilet bowl, forgotten.
Some days, swirled on bathtub enamel, observed.
This is an awe-filled love, a repeated devotion,
a liquid miracle collection.

Call it proof. Call it frailty. Call it unclean.
Call it mystical, virtuous, deprivation, mere biology —
this act is rehearsal.

This practice squat-and-push for future potential,
to ooze this life force, to heave and pour, then more,
into a whole body's worth. To sponge this red self
from that new being, uncover bright eyes, cradle tiny arms
someday.

For now, though, I am content with only the squish
of silicone. Only the musical red cell pour-and-splash
into ceramic bowl. Only the split-second dazed wonder
at this monthly, womanly, glory…

Sikiliza

i

July is baking this London balcony // Barcelona beach // Nairobi jacaranda-lined street // to sweltering // parked outside Johannesburg's Market Theatre // a London ambulance wailing // you hear *Vul'indlela* playing // someone swears in French // you are circling Geneva's three-legged chair // on Westlands roundabout a street kid named Moses begs for mandazi money // oyster card ready // a shirtless man calls you *guapisima* // *boerewors* and onions sizzling // the next train will arrive in 2 minutes // you bata for a Masai necklace // two kites swoop to seize your samosa // you swear in English // your friends are laughing in a nearby pub // tavern // *chiringuito* // there is always beer // the road is long and grey // to the left a sudden wall // red graffiti // 'You Are Here' //

ii

The scream of sirens wakes you nightly.
Here dead bees lie, forgotten prayers
on the pavement. Maybe disorientation
caused their death, same smoke that catches
in your throat, here, where *the next train*
to arrive at platform 8 will be — your descent
into madness. Only birds woke you in the home
before. Which home do we mean?
Here is anywhere you do not wish to be.
You ache for the scent of jasmine every day
until you have it, and then it's mosquitos
that bite you back into yearning for
silly Western things like app-dialled food
deliveries, fast internet speeds. It should
take less than 72 hours for relocated bees
to acclimatise. You don't even have jetlag to blame
for your grumpiness. Your mother wears
her emigrations like medallions,
tells you gratitude is the key
to happy. Her voice,
same resonant hum as honey,
thrums in seven languages.

iii

You aren't fluent / but / your tongue puzzles itself across three languages / ~~friends~~ ~~audio notes~~ *les notes audio d'amis* on repeat / a patchwork of comfort accents / ~~No~~ ~~matter~~ *No importa* where you are / home, ~~is somewhere else~~ *sio hapa* / 'Permanent settlement' ~~does not exist~~ *n'exist pas* / You are accustomed to being ~~misunderstood~~ *incomprendida* / choosing a binary sexuality feels like choosing ~~a home~~ *nyumba moja* / choosing one home feels like losing another / but you learn / ~~learn~~ *unajifunza* to ~~you name your body home~~ *llamas a tu cuerpo hogar* / Treat its many sensitivities as ~~sacred~~ *sacrée* / anoint the walls of your skin with ~~coconut oil~~ *mafuta ya nazi* / make it ritual / learn ~~your body's language~~ *le langage de ton corps* / ~~listen~~ *sikiliza* for your gut / pay ~~attention~~ *atención* to your blood / become cartographer of your states / ~~move~~ ~~to your own winds~~ *bougez à votre guise* / ~~Here~~ *Hapa* you are all that you need / ~~Here~~ ~~you can build~~ *aquí puedes construir* your own mosaic / ~~Here~~ *Icí* you need not / speak

Somewhere We Exist, Happy

Remember your hand warming my thigh?
  That 7-hour road trip, me blushing
    from the heat in your voice.

Or how we laughed, wheezing, and wide-mouthed,
  seal-clapping into kisses and kisses.

The way you breathed my name
  slow, in the amber light of your bedroom.

Somewhere, somehow,
  we are still singing to Nina Simone
    in a tangle of bedsheets,

  so deliriously off-key
I kiss you once more
    to be sure you are real.

Separate now, in this quiet solitude
  I want to believe
    our voices are still here, somewhere
    overflowing with all that joy.

A Theory of Everything

The woman yelling out daily
for you to buy the Big Issue
names all of us beautiful. We know
better. Still we blush and blink the sun
from our eyes. Men in dark suits,
women with flyaway hair and papers
stepping around so as not to look at her.
Look at us, the ever-evolving. Since
the first fish decided to try its luck
on land. Now a child screams
against the current of a waterslide.
There are trees still standing
who have witnessed world wars,
nodding patiently in the wind. Imagine
a section cut from one of them, rings
like a vinyl record playing what it knows.
All those echoes. The woman is pleading now.
I want to [   ]. There are so many wants
but I keep walking. Did you know, your great
great great great great great grandmother looks
just like mine? Apple cheeks rising to smile,
soft tree bark wrinkles. Praising freckles
as stars, she too, traced her lover's constellations.
In this light, my veins are lightning bolts.
Far below now, in the foundations of our houses
live families of mice we have not yet met,
alongside fleas and worms and spider silk,
worlds like Russian nesting dolls pressed
into one another. Here, look,
you are a child, chubby fisted
and giggling, one slow panorama
head-turn and you have grandchildren.
Watch how insistently we survive.
See how fragile we are.
Listen – there is so much more to say.

Notes

Sikiliza (Swahili) - to listen
Verb. -sikiliza (infinitive kusikiliza)
Causative form of -sikia: to listen.

Authors mentioned herein and the publications their referenced works can be found in:

Victoria Adukwei Bulley   - *Girl B*, 2017
Margaret Atwood   - *Alias Grace*, 1996
Sumia Jaama   - *For Those with Collages for Tongues:*
                                   Barbican Young Poets Anthology, 2018
Jake Wild Hall   - *Solomon's World*, 2017

Acknowledgements

I would like first to thank my emotional support systems who have held my heart in its most tender moments both as a person, and as a writer. I want to thank my mother, without whose unwavering emotional and financial support I would not have been able to continue writing. Your belief in me is my north star, Mama, thank you. Thank you to my sister, for your patient listening, your sage advice, your willingness to attend poetry events with me and to always offer feedback on baby poems.

Thank you to the many open mic nights across South Africa and the UK that I have had the joy of attending, performing at and learning from, for creating safe spaces to share and to grow and for your moments of true gratitude and guidance which have helped me trust my place on this creative path. Thank you to the first country I truly fell in love with, for holding and shaping and nurturing me; Kenya you're forever engraved in me.

Thank you to the many poetry collectives I have had the pleasure of being a part of: Scribe Writes, Write Up, the Roundhouse Poetry Collective, London Queer Writers, Apples and Snake's The Writers Room, and, of course, Barbican Young Poets. To every facilitator I have had the pleasure of being taught by, and to every poetry peer I have experienced electric moments with, thank you for all that you shared. Each poem in this collection is tethered in some way to lessons and inspirations from the people I have known and learnt from in these workshops.

Thank you to Nkosinathi Gaar, forever missed and forever treasured, my first inspiration. For your wit, your pizazz and your willingness to teach me. Thank you to Xabiso Vili, my most exciting and unpredictable competition, my favourite slam poet to lose to, and my very first unofficial poetry guide. May we continue reaching for the pen together, Heart.

Thank you to the loves and lovers that have imprinted on me. Here are the lighthouses I have made from and for the storms we could not weather.

And to the fierce, brave, loyal loves who remain, thank you. Here are my humble tributes and deep appreciations.

I am filled with gratitude for so many people who have influenced, supported, and believed in me over the years. But none perhaps more than Jacob Sam-La Rose, for teaching me not only how to hone my poetics, but also how to move through the world as more than just an exposed nerve. Without you, this collection would remain diary fragments tossed in a book bag and there is no telling where this sensitive heart would be.

Jacob, you have taught me more about poetry, about life, about the very practice of being a creative human than any other person I know. You have inspired, reassured, and challenged me as a mentor and as a friend over the years and so much of the way I am today can be traced back to thought-seeds you planted in some of our very first sessions together. Thank you for your precious time and patience, for your steadfast kindness, and for your dependable honesty.

Lastly, thank you to you, reader, for purchasing this collection. Thank you for your willingness to engage with my words and world(s), and for the deeply felt encouragement that your curiosity, support, and listening heart offer me.